"Experimental, obscure, timeless, essential, *venture of the infinite man*, published two years after his famous *Twenty Love Poems and a Song of Despair*, set Pablo Neruda on his course toward becoming the greatest poet in the history of the Spanish language. Its publication in English is a historic event, above all today, above all in this moment, above all, now." —RAÚL ZURITA, author of *Anteparaíso*

"In his early twenties and after the enormous success of *Twenty Love Poems and a Song of Despair*, Neruda surprised everyone by changing aesthetic gears in this book that was at once innovative and emblematic. The effort was part of what would ultimately become his ceaseless embrace of change as the sine qua non of style. Jessica Powell does wonders rendering these cantos for the first time into English, filling in a gap his legion of admirers will be thankful for. This isn't only an unseen Neruda but an unforeseen one too." —ILAN STAVANS, editor of *The Poetry of Pablo Neruda*

"What an act of generosity this book is. Eisner's introduction contextualizes and informs precisely as needed, and Jessica Powell's translation achieves astonishing beauty and refreshing truth. She has listened deeply to Neruda's text." —KATHERINE SILVER, translator

"Jessica Powell is the 'distant light that illuminates the fruit' of *venture of the infinite man*, the twenty-two-year-old Pablo Neruda's untranslated third book. One part quest and one part inner map, in Powell's hands the delicious and strange language of the original dances effortlessly in English. Readers can now experience the moment Neruda evolved from being only a brilliant singer of love poems into a maker of rich, stunning worlds. This book is a treasure." —TOMÁS Q. MORÍN, author of *Patient Zero*

"This book has the fascination of being Neruda becoming Neruda. It's the brilliant young poet who made himself famous at nineteen and twenty with *Twenty Love Poems*, beginning to absorb the lessons of the new surrealism and making his way to the world poet he would become in *Residence on Earth*. So it is a leap into the imagination of one of the crucial poets of the twentieth century as he is feeling his way." —ROBERT HASS, former U.S. Poet Laureate

venture
of the
infinite
man

Pablo Neruda

venture of the infinite man

Translated by Jessica Powell
With an Introduction by Mark Eisner

City Lights Books | San Francisco

First published in 1926 as *tentativa del hombre infinito* by Editorial Nascimento (Santiago, Chile).

Library of Congress Cataloging-in-Publication Data
Names: Neruda, Pablo, 1904-1973, author. | Ernst Powell, Jessica, translator.
  | Eisner, Mark, 1973- writer of introduction. | Neruda, Pablo, 1904-1973.
  Tentativa del hombre infinito. English. | Neruda, Pablo, 1904-1973.
  Tentativa del hombre infinito.
Title: Venture of the infinite man / Pablo Neruda ; translated by Jessica
  Powell ; introduction by Mark Eisner.
Description: San Francisco : City Lights Books, 2017. | In English and
  Spanish. | Poem.
Identifiers: LCCN 2017022444 | ISBN 9780872867192 (hardback)
Subjects: | BISAC: POETRY / Caribbean & Latin American.
Classification: LCC PQ8097.N4 T413 2017 | DDC 861/.62--dc23
LC record available at https://lccn.loc.gov/2017022444

City Lights Books are published at the City Lights Bookstore
261 Columbus Avenue, San Francisco, CA 94133
www.citylights.com

INTRODUCTION

In Santiago, Chile, 1925, a twenty-one-year-old poet named Pablo Neruda found himself at a crossroads. Despite the sensational success of his second book, the widely celebrated *Twenty Love Poems and a Song of Despair*, published just a year before, Neruda was in sad shape. "Pablo's state of mind was anxious, disconcerted," his friend Rubén Azócar noted. "It seemed to me that his soul was spinning around itself, seeking its own center. . . . [He] wanted to renew himself in some way, to examine himself from a different dimension."[1]

This desire for self-exploration, the craving for new perspectives through which he might ground himself, led Neruda to experiment once again with his style. Despite the love poems' unique potency, he was already determined to break with their lyrical realism, with poetry's traditional forms in general. His intention was to "strip poetry of all its objectiveness and to say what I have to say in the most serious form possible."[2]

What resulted was his discovery of a unique form, representing a stark stylistic departure from the love poems. Most strikingly, he discarded rhyme, meter, punctuation and capitalization in an attempt to better replicate the subconscious voice, to, in his words, bring his poetry even closer to "irreducible purity, the closest approximation to naked thought, to the intimate labor of the soul."[3] Indeed, he rejected capitalization even in the title of the book that would be the result of his experiment: *tentativa del hombre infinito* (*venture of the infinite man*).

venture of the infinite man, first published in 1926, just two years after *Twenty Love Poems*, is an avant-garde lyrical narrative, comprised of fifteen uniquely composed, but intimately linked, cantos. They are spread over forty-four pages, divided up and placed on each page in an inconsistent but not random fashion, the spacing serving as an element of the oneiric book. As if to signal that the book was not a compilation of disparate pieces, but a single unified work, the poet announced in large red type directly after the title page that this was a "Poem by Pablo Neruda."

Though Neruda would later call *venture* "one of the most important books of my poetry," the work failed to garner the critical and popular reception he had been hoping for. Indeed, in 1950, twenty-five years after he finished writing it, Neruda noted that *venture* was "the least read and least studied of all my work,"[4] a lament that, unfortunately, holds true today. *venture* has continued to be passed over, primarily because of its heavy avant-garde experimentalism, which, on the one hand, makes it so exceptional and rich, yet on the other, has caused critics and publishers (and translators) to shy away from its unconventional form.

As René de Costa wrote in his seminal book, *The Poetry of Pablo Neruda*, "Critics who liked his love poetry were at first dismayed by this book, for in it Neruda seemed to have abandoned not only rhyme and meter but also, according to some, any semblance of meaning. The problem was that in his desire to purify his poetic language, to rid it entirely of the hollow rhetoric of the past, he created a work that was so strange and unfamiliar to most readers of the time that they were unable and unwilling to make any sense out of it."[5]

The critics' bewilderment, which extended even to Neruda's own friends, was emblematic of the book's reception. One of the most influential reviewers referred to it as "going the way of the absurd."[6] Another, Raúl Silva Castro, who had been the very first to publish Neruda in the Chilean Student Federation's journal, complained: "The flesh and blood we had admired so much in the author's other books are missing here. . . . [A reader] might just as well begin to read from the back as from the front, or even the middle. One would understand the same, that is to say, very little."[7]

These early critics and readers were completely thrown

off by the experimental nature of *venture*. Was there actually supposed to be a cohesive arc across this whole "poem," as Neruda was calling it, or were these just unrelated strips of dream-like images? Was there any substance to it? Was it even poetry? They just couldn't grasp it, for, as de Costa notes, "Most readers in 1926 reacted, quite naturally, to what *tentativa* did not have. The book's so-called 'formlessness' was then most disturbing; even the pages were unnumbered."

Readers today are in a better position to appreciate its true achievement, to "see it for what it actually does contain." In fact, in 1975, fifty years after Neruda finished the poem, René de Costa, at that time a professor of Spanish at the University of Chicago, published an article calling for a "reappraisal" of *venture of the infinite man*. He argued that while the book's "unfamiliar manner of presentation once obscured the meaning of Neruda's avant-garde literature from all but the initiated," today, we are more enabled and evolved as readers.[8] Thus, in viewing the book now from a postvanguard perspective, "it should be possible to ascertain [its] expressive system and to perceive in it something more than the verbal chaos which so alarmed its early critics."

One of the more remarkable characteristics of Neruda's work throughout his life was its constant evolution. Aside from the inherent poetic qualities of this pivotal book, readers of this edition will be able to experience one of the most striking examples of Neruda's growth as a poet. As de Costa has noted, "It was only after abandoning the hollow shell of rhyme and meter and freeing his expression from the logical concatenation of continuous discourse that he was able to attain the unusual inner cohesion and high degree of poetic tension which stylistically link the hermetic text of 1926 [*tentativa*] to the expressive system of the *Residencia* cycle."[9]

Indeed, the first poems of his next book, *Residence on Earth* (*Residencia en la tierra*), drew on Neruda's unique approach to surrealism, displaying a groundbreaking use of expressive symbols and images. And that work redefined Spanish poetry, its influence reverberating around the globe for generations. This is the most important result of Neruda's experimentation with *venture*: he had set forth to construct a new style and, in doing so, built the essential poetic infrastructure that served as the bridge between the blockbuster plain lyricism of *Twenty Love Poems* and his unprecedented, landmark *Residence on Earth*. Neruda himself saw this book as crucial to his evolution as a poet: "I have always looked upon *venture of the infinite man* as one of the real nuclei of my poetry," he said at the age of fifty, "because working on those poems, in those now distant years, I was acquiring a consciousness that I didn't have before, and if my expressions, their clarity or mystery, are anywhere measured, it is in this extraordinarily personal little book. . . . Within its smallness and minimal expression, more than most of my works . . . it claimed, it secured, the path that I had to follow."[10]

Neruda's fondness for this book, and his assertion of its centrality to his work as a whole, make the fact that it has been so largely overlooked even more remarkable. The neglect has compromised readers' access to it. While the poem has been included within some compilations and anthologies, until recently, the only stand-alone edition published in Spanish since its original 1926 release was a limited edition, released in honor of Neruda's fiftieth birthday in 1964. A "commemorative" edition to celebrate the ninetieth anniversary of the initial publication was published by the Pablo Neruda Foundation in 2016, but in a limited printing sold only in the gift shop at Neruda's old house in Santiago, which the Foundation runs as a museum. And, at the time of this writing, an "academic" Spanish edition annotated by Hernán Loyola is set to be released in 2017. A complete translation of the work into English has never been published in book form—until now, that is.

Furthermore, perhaps because of how strange the original was, no version printed since 1926 has ever exactly replicated that first edition (with the exception of the Neruda Foundation's small 2016 commemorative printing). Rather, they contain substantial changes in page and line breaks, as well as the spacing and location of lines on the page, elements that are crucial to any poetic text, especially this one, as they greatly affect the intelligibility and meaning of the individual cantos as well as their interrelated cohesion. These versions also usually include changes, or "corrections," to Neruda's original wording and spelling. The original text includes typos and misprints that Neruda did not want to correct. According to Neruda, when his publisher—who had supported the vanguard venture, both emotionally and materially—showed him the advance page proofs in January 1925, he made the decision not to correct the errata:

To my delight, I saw an abundance of errors that pal-
pitated among my verses. Instead of correcting them
I returned the proofs intact to don Carlos who, sur-
prised, said, "No mistakes?"

"There are and I'm leaving them," I responded.[11]

Just as Neruda intentionally eschewed capitalization and
punctuation marks,* by leaving in these natural slips he felt he
was emulating the unmediated, free-flowing articulation of the
subconscious.

And so, until now, René de Costa's call for a reapprais-
al, for a re-issue of *tentativa* for the contemporary reader, had

---

* Neruda did use accent marks, however in several instances they were
missing in the original printing. Because the presence or absence of an
accent mark in a given word in Spanish can change its meaning, and
as such, drastically impact the translation, we have chosen to insert the
missing accents for our edition.

gone unanswered. I visited him in Chicago in 2004, both of us participating in events around the city celebrating Neruda's centennial that year. There was a lot to talk about, but I found our conversations about *venture* particularly passionate and salient. I left confident in my appraisal of the book's seminality; we agreed that it was a shame that there was no English translation available, nor even an accessible Spanish edition. As it is such an avant-garde book, I proposed the project to the vanguard publisher, City Lights. Lawrence Ferlinghetti dug it immediately, and the press soon became excited about the publishing possibilities, as much for the book's inherent poetic richness as for its important place in global literary history. When City Lights publisher Elaine Katzenberger agreed to take on the project, I asked my friend, translator Jessica Powell, to take on the daunting task of rendering this incredibly challenging text in English.

Through her brilliant effort, readers of English are now

able to experience this important work for the very first time, and in an edition in which we have taken pains to respect the original 1926 edition, from its lack of punctuation and capital letters, to its line and page breaks and the errata (with the exception of the aforementioned accent marks) that Neruda consciously decided to leave in the manuscript. Even our cover emulates the spare avant-garde aesthetic of the original edition. With this first-ever English translation of the complete work, a new readership can walk through Neruda's semi-surrealistic stretch of the poetic void.

Our edition is bilingual, our aim being to present the poem in Spanish exactly how Neruda intended it, while also offering an English translation that will make the text accessible to English-only readers. The native Spanish speaker can enjoy the poem just as Neruda wrote it, though we urge even those not fluent in Spanish to read at least some of the original lines to get a feel for the sounds and rhythms of the poem.

Especially with a work as tricky as this one, some of these will inevitably be lost in translation, despite Jessica Powell's painstaking craft in capturing them. So, even if one does not understand the exact meaning of the Spanish, the original sounds and rhythms can be sensed, which is especially important with this work and its integral relationship with the voice of the subconscious.

It must also be said that even a native Spanish speaker may find parts of this work perplexing or even unintelligible, and again, Powell has carefully preserved this "strangeness" in the English translation. Many of the phrasings seem unusual, illogical, surrealistic, because that was Neruda's intent. His aim was for us to hear the tone, the linguistic mechanism of the subconscious; we can't expect to understand its every image. Instead, if we are aware of what we are getting into, if we accept, for instance, that in some places where we'd expect a comma separating a phrase there won't be one, we can allow our minds to simply slip over it. With this book, if you release the need to understand everything rationally, what to others may seem "the way of the absurd" will became an epic cinematic voyage through an imaginary dimension, dreamed up through the creative genius of one of the most important poets of the twentieth century.

⌒⌒

venture of the infinite man was written over a two-year period in which Neruda had begun practicing his own form of "automatic writing," dipping into some of the techniques and tenets of surrealism, but not steeping his poetry in them completely. As André Breton wrote in the *Surrealist Manifesto*, surrealism "is based on the belief in the superior reality of certain forms of previously neglected associations." It stressed the "omnipotence of dream" and the "disinterested play of thought."[12]

Yet, as de Costa highlights, while Breton and other surrealists wanted to capture the voice of the subconscious, Neruda only wanted to emulate its style. In *venture*, instead of simply delivering a deluge of language, he added some clarity through premeditated composition following the spontaneity. He reviewed and revised the words, creating conscious constructions and recurring themes.

While the first reviews of the book charged Neruda with writing out of control, it only seemed that way. In fact, frustrated by the critics' failure to grasp his method, he went to his friend Raúl Silva Castro, whose review of the book in Santiago's largest newspaper had expressed his complete inability to penetrate the poem. During their conversation, Neruda stressed that he needed to clear out the clunky, impure elements of his poetry for it to function as he desired, even if this might make it less comprehensible to the casual reader:

Even proper names seem false to me, an element foreign to poetry. In the first fragment of *venture* there's a verse that says: "only one immobile star its blue phosphorous." At first I had put: "only one star Sirius its blue phosphorous," but I had to take the name out of there: Sirius, which was very precise.

But the name was too "objective," it was an unpoetic element in the poem.[13]

Neruda's explanations eventually convinced Silva Castro of *venture*'s artistic merit. Where in his first review he had dismissed his friend's book for its formlessness, now he described how Neruda had gotten rid of "the dead weight of rhyme and rhythm" and the "unnecessary separation of functions for capital and lower-case letters." "Is this poetry?" he asked. "Of course it is. But it is a new kind of poetry."[14]

Any attempt to analyze precisely what takes place in the poem will be complicated by the fact that, as we have noted, it is likely impossible to understand everything on a purely rational level. Conceptually, while Neruda's writing process may have been less "pure" than surrealism's "pure psychic automatism," *venture*'s narrative and textured imagery does align with the movement's desire to resolve the "seemingly contradictory states" of dream and reality "into a kind of absolute reality, a surreality."[15] In fact, *venture*'s plot revolves around its protagonist's search for absolute wholeness, a new reality, a restored consciousness, a quest that mirrors Neruda's own search for self-discovery and expression.

Neruda was twenty when he first started writing *venture*; at the beginning of the book we learn that the poem's subject is "a man of twenty." We see this young man with his "soul in despair." This is the same state in which his friend Rubén found Neruda just before he began writing *venture*, his soul "spinning around itself, seeking its own center." It is also the same state that defines the "Song of Despair" at the end of the *Twenty Love Poems*, the last pages Neruda published before *venture* (in fact, a great deal of the imagery in the "Song of Despair" suggests that *venture* starts where that song left off).

In this poem, Neruda describes the fantastic, nocturnal voyage of a melancholic Infinite Man who sets off on a quest to rediscover himself, to reach a state of pure consciousness. Throughout this quest for self-transformation, Neruda has the poem's speaker refer to himself in the first, second and third person — sometimes suddenly shifting from one to another in the same canto. The changing point of view enhances the illusionary effect of the book, adding elements of suspenseful uncertainty, as well as adding a new dimension to the sense of time — as we travel on this journey, when he references himself as "you," it seems to signal that he's referring to himself in the past, a person from whom he's moving away — as in, that *was* you.[16] By the end, though, the Man consistently speaks in the first person, emphasizing his presence in the present, a new self-recognition and assuredness as he completes the quest, having conquered the night and been delivered from the void: "i am standing in the light." (An additional difficulty arises from the fact that night, dream, the reality of day are all personified characters within the poem, whom Neruda also refers to from varying points of view, provoking doubt as to who is who.)

In the opening canto, Neruda depicts an almost cinematic tapestry of the nocturnal void through which the man will travel. To start, he "shattered my heart like a mirror in order to walk through myself" (like Alice with her looking glass).[17] Now he can travel through night, trying to conquer it, so that he can achieve that absolute oneness he seeks. In a mid-book climax, he achieves physical union during a sexual experience with night, personified as a woman. He becomes one with the night.[18]

Following the ecstasy of this encounter, he is released from his melancholy, enlivened: "i surprise myself i sing delirious under the big top / like a lovestruck tightrope walker." He has tapped into his poetic ability, and he begins to meditatively seek his inner self: "letting the sky in deeply watching the sky i am thinking" . . . "i began to speak to myself in a low voice."

And while, by the final canto, it seems that the he has completed his quest ("i am standing in the light like midday on earth / i want to tell it all with tenderness"), the completion of the book brought no personal resolution to the trio of problems with which Rubén had noticed his friend struggling: "love, money, and poetry." Yet, regardless of its disheartening reception at the time of publication, the experience of writing *venture* would have its rewards. When we read *venture* today, Neruda's poetic vision seems almost prophetic. At one moment, the speaker, holding the night in an intimate embrace, speaks to himself: "something that does not belong to you descends from your head / and fills your raised hand with gold." It is as if a new poetic power created by the process of writing *venture* fell into his hand, illuminating it with new skills and visions with which he would then compose the immersive, extraordinary and moving poems at the beginning of his classic *Residence on Earth*. His voyage with (or through) the *venture of the infinite man* was the experience that got him there.

Mark Eisner, 2017

NOTES

1. Rubén Azócar. "Testimonio," *Revista Aurora*, no. 3-4 (1964): 215.

2. Raúl Silva Castro. "Una hora de charla con Pablo Neruda." *El Mercurio* (Santiago), Oct. 10, 1926.

3. Pablo Neruda. "Erratas y erratones," *Ercilla*, no. 1 (1969): 784. In Neruda's *Obras Completas V*, ed. Hernán Loyola (Barcelona: Galaxia Gutenberg, 2002), 237.

4. In conversation with Cardona Peña. Alfredo Cardona Peña. "Pablo Neruda: Breve Historia de sus Libros," *Cuadernos Americanos* 54, no. 6 (1950): 265.

5. René de Costa. *The Poetry of Pablo Neruda* (Cambridge, Mass: Harvard University Press, 1979), 4.

6. "Tentativa del hombre infinito, por Pablo Neruda," *La Nación* (Santiago), January 10, 1926.

7. Cited by René de Costa in *The Poetry of Pablo Neruda*, 42.

8. Pablo Neruda. "Algunas reflexiones improvisadas sobre mis trabajos" (speech given at Chile's Biblioteca Nacional de Santiago), *Mapocho* 2, no. 3

(1964). In Neruda's *Obras Completas IV*, ed. Hernán Loyola (Barcelona: Galaxia Gutenberg, 2001), 1204.

9. René de Costa. "Pablo Neruda's Tentativa del hombre infinito: Notes for a reappraisal," *Modern Philology* 73, no. 2 (1976): 146–147.

10. Neruda. "Algunas reflexiones improvisadas sobre mis trabajos."

11. Neruda. "Erratas y erratones," 237–238.

12. André Breton. "Manifesto of Surrealism" (1924), in *Manifestoes of Surrealism* (Ann Arbor: University of Michigan Press, 1969), 26.

13. Silva Castro. "Una hora de charla con Pablo Neruda."

14. Ibid.

15. Breton. "Manifesto of Surrealism," 26.

16. Hernán Loyola. "Lectura de Tentativa del hombre infinito de Pablo Neruda," *Revista Iberoamericana* 49, no. 123-124 (1983): 377.

17. Wilson, Jason. *A Companion to Pablo Neruda: Evaluating Neruda's Poetry.* (Woodbridge, Suffolk, UK: Tamesis, 2008), 85.

18. René de Costa. *The Poetry of Pablo Neruda*, 53.

venture
of the
infinite
m a n

A POEM BY
PABLO NERUDA

pale blazes twisting at the edge of night
dead smoke invisible dust clouds race

black forges slumbering behind nightfallen hills
the sadness of man cast into the arms of sleep

city from the hills at night the harvesters sleep
indistinct in the final flames
but you are there fixed to your horizon
like a boat at the dock ready to set sail I believe
before the dawn

death rattle tree candelabra of old flames
distant fire my heart is sad

only one immobile star its blue phosphorous
the movements of the night stagger toward the sky

city from the hills through the leafy night
a yellow stain its face parts the shadow
while stretched out in the grass i search
there they pass by blazing i alone alive

stretched out in the grass my heart is sad
the blue moon claws climbs floods

emissary you went happily along in the falling evening
dusk rolled on extinguishing flowers

stretched out in the grass made of black clover
and its delirious passion only wavers

gather a dewy butterfly as a necklace
bind me with your belt of striving stars

oh coiled thickets towards which sleep advances trains
oh mound of enthusiastic earth where i stand sobbing
vertebrae of the night distant water restless wind you break
and stars crucified behind the mountain

its momentum rising a wing passes by a flight oh night without keys
oh night of mine in my hour in my furious and aching hour
it lifted me like seaweed on a wave
receive my wretched heart
when you enfold the animals in sleep
crisscross it with your vast straps of silence
it is at your feet awaiting a departure
because you hold it face to face with yourself night of black spirals
and may all the strength inside it be fertile
tied to the sky with stars of rain
procreate lash yourself to that prow blue minerals
embarked on that nocturnal voyage
a man of twenty holds fast to a frantic rein
it's that he wanted to go off in pursuit of the night
between his hungering hands the wind startles

star suspended between the thick night the days of tall sails
as between you and your shadow uncertainties lie down to sleep
dock of doubts dancer on a string you held up twilights
you had in secret a dead man like a lonely road

beholding you then the bold ones leap forth you climb to the lights
                                                    [migrating
who gathers in the line empty boardwalks and fog
your breakwater of aching metals face down at the water's edge time
                                                    [pursuing you
the night of emeralds and mills turns the night of emeralds and mills
what do you desire now you are alone sentinel
you ran to the shore of the country looking for it
like the sleepwalker at the edge of his dream
draw near when the bells awaken you
bridle the temperatures with hopes and sorrows

i twist this hostile undergrowth this rocking chair for birds
distracted emissary oh solitude i want to sing

solitude of difficult darkness my hungering soul stumbles
train of light way up there a being without memories assaults you

i claw this bark i destroy the stalks of grass
and the night invades the tunnel like wine

savage wind hollower of the sky let us howl
my soul in despair and in joy who is knocking

facing the inaccessible a limitless presence passes before you
you will mark out the paths like the crosses of the dead

prow mast leaf in the storm desolation drives you on with no return
you look like the ruined tree and the water that shatters it

where it continues along its cold rails
and the night animal stops but does not rest

i do not know how to sing of the daytime
without meaning to i let loose the canto the exaltation of the night
the wind blew past whipping my back happy emerging from its egg
stars descend to drink from the ocean

big ships of embers twist their green sails
why even say it so small that you hide sing little one
the planets turn like lively spindles they twirl
the heart of the world retracts and stretches
with the resolve of a spine and the cold fury of feathers
oh the rural silences studded with stars
i remember the eyes falling into that inverted well
toward which ascended the solitude of all frightened noises
the heedlessness of beasts sleeping upon their hard lilies
then i filled the heights with black butterflies medusa butterfly
commotion dampness fog appeared
and turned to the wall i wrote
oh night dead hurricane your dark lava slides
my joys bite into your ink
my joyous human song suckles your hard breasts
my human heart scales your wires
impatient i restrain my heart that dances
dances in the winds that cleanse you of your color
spellbound dancer on great tides that raise the dawn

twisting to that side or beyond you continue being mine
in the solitude of dusk your smile knocks
in that instant vines climb to my window
wind from high above lashes the hunger for your presence

a gesture of joy a word of sorrow that i were closer to you
on its profound clock night secludes hours
yet having you in my arms i hesitated
something that does not belong to you descends from your head
and fills your raised hand with gold

it is there between two walls in the distance
radiant wheels of stone hold up the day all the while
then hung from the gallows of twilight
it treads on the bell towers and the women in the villages
moving along the edge of my nets
beloved woman in my breast your dark head
in great sudden blazes the mill churns
and the hours of night fall like bats from the sky

somewhere else far far away you and i exist akin to ourselves
you inscribe daisies on the lonely earth
for that country truly belongs to us
dawn flies from our house

when i draw the sky near with my hands to fully awaken
damp clods of earth a tangled net breaks free
your kisses stick like snails to my back
the calendar year spins and days slip from the world like leaves

every time every time to the north are the unfinished cities
now the wet south sad crossroads
where fish mobile as scissors
ah you alone appear in my space in my ring
beside my photograph like the word ailing
behind you i place a family ill fated
radiant mine i leap belonging hour of my distraction
your relatives are stooped over and you calmly
behold yourself in a tear you dry your eyes where i was
it is raining suddenly my door is going to open

right beside me young woman in love
who else but you like the drunken wire is a song with no title
ah my sad one a smile spreads like a butterfly across your face
and for you my sister does not dress in black

i am the one who plucks names and high constellations of dew
in the night of blue walls high upon your brow
to sing your praises word of pure wings
the one who broke his fate always where he was not
for example the night rolling among silver crosses
that was your first kiss why even remember it
i spread you out before the silence
my earth the birds of my thirst protect you
and i kiss your mouth wet with twilight

it is farther away higher
to symbolize you i would grow a stalk of wheat
distracted heart twisted toward a wound
you halt the color of the night and liberate the prisoners

oh why did they stretch out the earth
from the side where I gaze at you and you are not there my little girl
between shadow and shadow shipwreck fate
i have nothing oh solitude

and yet you are the distant light that illuminates the fruit
and we shall die together
to think that you are there white ship ready to depart
and that we have our hands joined at the prow ship forever voyaging

this is my house
perfumed even now by the forests
from which they carted it away
there i shattered my heart like a mirror in order to walk through myself

that is the high window and there are the doors
whose was the axe that felled the trees
perhaps the wind hung its profound sorrow
from the rafters then left it behind
that was when the night danced among its nets
when the boy awoke sobbing
i do not tell i say in wretched words
even now the scaffolds split the twilight
and behind the glass the light of the oil lamp
it was for looking up at the sky
the rain was falling in petals of glass
there you followed the path that led into the tempest
just as the high insistence of the sea
isolates the hard rocks of the shoreline from the air
what did you want what did you suppose as if dying many times
all things rise to a great silence
and he despaired leaning at its edge
you held a painful flower
days spun among its petals daisies from dispirited pilots

dispirited vacant did you wrest from the shadows
the metal of the farthest distances or were you awaiting the shift
it dawned regardless on the earth's clocks
suddenly the days scale the years
here is your heart walking you are tired holding yourself up
at your side the birds bid farewell to the absent season

letting the sky in deeply watching the sky i am thinking
sitting uncertainly on that edge
oh sky woven with water and paper
i began to speak to myself in a low voice determined not to leave

drawn down by the breath of my roots
immobile ship hungering for those blue leagues
you were trembling and the fish began to pursue you
you burst out singing magnificent you wanted to sing
you wanted to sing sitting in your room that day
but the air in your heart was cold like inside a bell
a delirious rope was going to shatter your cold
my leg fell asleep in that position and i spoke to it
singing to it my soul is mine
the sky was a drop that rang out falling in the great solitude
i listen and time like a eucalyptus
sings frenetically from side to side
as if a thief were whistling inside it
ah and at the borderline i stopped horse of the canyons
skittish anxious motionless not urinating
in that instant i swear oh eventide you arrive a satisfied fisherman
your basket vivid in the dimming sky

for whom did i buy the solitude i possess tonight
who gives the order that quickens the pace
of the wind flower of the cold among unfinished leaves
if you call to me storm you thunder as distant as a train

sad wave fallen at my feet who calls you
sleepwalker of blood setting out each time in search of the dawn

i recognize you but far away remote
leaning into your eyes I seek the lost anchor
you hold it there ornate in mother-of-pearl arms
it is to end to never continue
and that is why i praise you disciple of my soul looking back at you
i seek you every time among the symbols of return
you are full of birds sleeping like the silence of the forests
heavy and sad lily you look off toward some other place
when i speak to you so distant you wound me woman of mine
step up the pace step up the pace and ignite the fireflies

i see a bee circling this bee does not exist now
small fly with red legs while each time in flight you strike
i duck my head helplessly
i follow a cord that marks at least a presence an ordinary experience

i hear the silence adorn itself with successive waves
turn return confused echoes then i sing out loud
shadow of stars rise up upon the brow of a man at the bend in a road
who carries on his back a pale woman of gold who looks like herself
all is lost the weeks are darkened
i see the wind turn with a certain purpose
like a flower that must release its perfume
i open the taciturn autumn i visit the site of the shipwrecks
in the depths of the sky the birds appear then like letters
and the dawn barely visible like the skin of a fruit
or is it that you submerge your feet then in another distance
the day is made of fire and is buttressed by its colors
the sea filled with green sails its froth whispers i am the sea
the movement beckoned the restless box
i have refreshed my soul with every breath
there i smother beside the antarctic nights
i don the moon like a hyacinth flower dampened by my doleful tear
i am sated and my life moves along its feet all in parallel

i beget fright i am filled with transparent terror
i am alone in a room with no windows
no longer bound by wandering routes
i see the walls fill up with snails like the sides of ships
i press my face to them deeply entranced
following a clock not loving the night i want it to pass
with its woven snake of lights
garland of chills my belt wraps around and around
i am the mare that gallops alone hopelessly in pursuit of the dawn so
                                                              [very sad
endless hole when i go along with my deafness trembling
people lying in their beds jump like rubber bands or fish
my wings swell with oblivion like the gazebo in a park
the harbors at daybreak like abandoned horseshoes
ah i surprise myself i sing delirious under the big top
like a lovestruck tightrope walker or the first fisherman
poor man trembling like a drop you isolate
a square of time perfectly still

the month of june stretched out suddenly in time with seriousness
                                    [and exactitude
like a horse and on a lightning bolt i crossed over the edge
ah the crackling of the peaceful air was very great
the empty cinemas the color of cemeteries

the ruined ships the sorrows
above the foliage
above the cows' horns the night taut its sail dancing
the quick movement of the day like that of hands halting a vehicle
frightened i was eating
oh rain you grow like the plants oh victrolas lost in thought
people of eager heart i celebrated it all
on a train of satisfactions my portrait
backdropped by the world that i describe with passion
the trees interesting as newspapers the villages the railroad tracks
ah the gloomy place where the rainbow
leaves its long skirt entangled upon fleeing
the poets the philosophers the couples in love
i begin to celebrate it all humble enthusiast
i have the joy of a contented baker and then
it dawned weakly the color of a violin
with the sound of a bell with the scent of long distances

give me back the great rose the thirst brought to the world
where i am going i suppose things are the same
the night important and sad and therein my complaint
barcarolero of the long waters when

suddenly a seagull grows upon your brow my heart is weary
mark me your gray foot laden with distance
your journey from the shore of the bitter sea oh wait for me
the mist awakens like a violet it's that
a boy climbs up your tree beloved night
to steal your fruit
and the lizards spring from your heavy vestments
then the day leaps upon its bee
i am standing in the light like midday on earth
i want to tell it all with tenderness
sentinel of bitter seasons there you are
restless fisherman let me adorn you for example
a belt of fruit sweet melancholy
wait for me where i am going ah twilight
dinner barcaroles from the sea oh wait for me
overtaking you like a shout falling behind you like a footprint oh
                                                    [wait

sitting in that final shadow or still later
still

tentativa
d   e   l
hombre
infinito

POEMA DE
PABLO NERUDA

hogueras pálidas revolviéndose al borde de las noches
corren humos difuntos polvaredas invisibles

fraguas negras durmiendo detrás de los cerros anochecidos
la tristeza del hombre tirada entre los brazos del sueño

ciudad desde los cerros en la noche los segadores duermen
debatida a las últimas hogueras
pero estás allí pegada a tu horizonte
como una lancha al muelle lista para zarpar lo creo
antes del alba

árbol de estertor candelabro de llamas viejas
distante incendio mi corazón está triste

sólo una estrella inmóvil su fósforo azul
los movimientos de la noche aturden hacia el cielo

ciudad desde los cerros entre la noche de hojas
mancha amarilla su rostro abre la sombra
mientras tendido sobre el pasto deletreo
ahí pasan ardiendo sólo yo vivo

tendido sobre el pasto mi corazón está triste
la luna azul araña trepa inunda

emisario ibas alegre en la tarde que caía
el crepúsculo rodaba apagando flores

tendido sobre el pasto hecho de tréboles negros
y tambalea sólo su pasión delirante

recoge una mariposa húmeda como un collar
anúdame tu cinturón de estrellas esforzadas

oh matorrales crespos adonde el sueño avanza trenes
oh montón de tierra entusiasta donde de pie sollozo
vértebras de la noche agua tan lejos viento intranquilo rompes
también estrellas crucificadas detrás de la montaña

alza su empuje un ala pasa un vuelo oh noche sin llaves
oh noche mía en mi hora en mi hora furiosa y doliente
eso me levantaba como la ola al alga
acoge mi corazón desventurado
cuando rodeas los animales del sueño
crúzalo con tus vastas correas de silencio
está a tus pies esperando una partida
porque lo pones cara a cara a ti misma noche de hélices negras
y que toda fuerza en él sea fecunda
atada al cielo con estrellas de lluvia
procrea tú amárrate a esa proa minerales azules
embarcado en ese viaje nocturno
un hombre de veinte años sujeta una rienda frenética
es que él quería ir a la siga de la noche
entre sus manos ávidas el viento sobresalta

estrella retardada entre la noche gruesa los días de altas velas
como entre tú y tu sombra se acuestan las vacilaciones
embarcadero de las dudas bailarín en el hilo sujetabas crepúsculos
tenías en secreto un muerto como un camino solitario

divisándote entonces resaltan las audaces te trepas a las luces
[emigrando
quien recoge el cordel vacíos malecones y la niebla
tu espigón de metales dolientes de bruces al borde de las aguas el
[tiempo persiguiéndote
la noche de esmeraldas y molinos se da vueltas la noche de esme-
[raldas y molinos

que deseas ahora estás solo centinela
corrías a la orilla del país buscándolo
como el sonámbulo al borde de su sueño
aproxímate cuando las campanas te despierten
ataja las temperaturas con esperanzas y dolores

tuerzo esta hostil maleza mecedora de los pájaros
emisario distraído oh soledad quiero cantar

soledad de tinieblas difíciles mi alma hambrienta tropieza
tren de luz allá arriba te asalta un ser sin recuerdos

araño esta corteza destrozo los ramales de la hierba
y la noche como vino invade el túnel

salvaje viento socavador del cielo ululemos
mi alma en desesperanza y en alegría quien golpea

frente a lo inaccesible por ti pasa una presencia sin límites
señalarás los caminos como las cruces de los muertos

proa mástil hoja en el temporal te empuja el abandono sin regreso
te pareces al árbol derrotado y al agua que lo estrella

donde lo sigue su riel frío
y se para sin muchas treguas el animal de la noche

no sé hacer el canto de los días
sin querer suelto el canto la alabanza de las noches
pasó el viento latigándome la espalda alegre saliendo de su huevo
descienden las estrellas a beber al océano

tuercen sus velas verdes grandes buques de brasa
para qué decir eso tan pequeño que escondes canta pequeño
los planetas dan vuelta como husos entusiastas giran
el corazón del mundo se repliega y se estira
con voluntad de columna y fría furia de plumas
oh los silencios campesinos claveteados de estrellas
recuerdo los ojos caían en ese pozo inverso
hacia dónde ascendía la soledad de todos los ruidos espantados
el descuido de las bestias durmiendo sus duros lirios
preñé entonces la altura de mariposas negras mariposa medusa
aparecían estrépitos humedad nieblas
y vuelto a la pared escribí
oh noche huracán muerto resbala tu obscura lava
mis alegrías muerden tus tintas
mi alegre canto de hombre chupa tus duras mamas
mi corazón de hombre se trepa por tus alambres
exasperado contengo mi corazón que danza
danza en los vientos que limpian tu color
bailador asombrado en las grandes mareas que hacen surgir el alba

torciendo hacia ese lado o más allá continúas siendo mía
en la soledad del atardecer golpea tu sonrisa
en ese instante trepan enredaderas a mi ventana
el viento de lo alto cimbra la sed de tu presencia

un gesto de alegría una palabra de pena que estuviera más cerca de ti
en su reloj profundo la noche aísla horas
sin embargo teniéndote entre los brazos vacilé
algo que no te pertenece desciende de tu cabeza
y se te llena de oro la mano levantada

hay esto entre dos paredes a lo lejos
radiantes ruedas de piedra sostienen el día mientras tanto
después colgado en la horca del crepúsculo
pisa en los campanarios y en las mujeres de los pueblos
moviéndose en la orilla de mis redes
mujer querida en mi pecho tu cabeza cerrada
a grandes llamaradas el molino se revuelve
y caen las horas nocturnas como murciélagos del cielo

en otra parte lejos lejos existen tú y yo parecidos a nosotros
tú escribes margaritas en la tierra solitaria
es que ese país de cierto nos pertenece
el amanecer vuela de nuestra casa

cuando aproximo el cielo con las manos para despertar completamente
sus húmedos terrones su red confusa se suelta
tus besos se pegan como caracoles a mi espalda
gira el año de los calendarios y salen del mundo los días como hojas

cada vez cada vez al norte están las ciudades inconclusas
ahora el sur mojado encrucijada triste
en donde los peces movibles como tijeras
ah sólo tú apareces en mi espacio en mi anillo
al lado de mi fotografía como la palabra está enfermo
detrás de ti pongo una familia desventajosa
radiante mía salto perteneciente hora de mi distracción
están encorvados tus parientes y tú con tranquilidad
te miras en una lágrima te secas los ojos donde estuve
está lloviendo de repente mi puerta se va a abrir

al lado de mí mismo señorita enamorada
quién sino tú como el alambre ebrio es una canción sin título
ah triste mía la sonrisa se extiende como una mariposa en tu rostro
y por ti mi hermana no viste de negro

yo soy el que deshoja nombres y altas constelaciones de rocío
en la noche de paredes azules alta sobre tu frente
para alabarte a ti palabra de alas puras
el que rompió su suerte siempre donde no estuvo
por ejemplo en la noche rodando entre cruces de plata
que fue tu primer beso para qué recordarlo
yo te puse extendida delante del silencio
tierra mía los pájaros de mi sed te protegen
y te beso la boca mojada con crepúsculo

es más allá más alto
para significarte criaría una espiga
corazón distraído torcido hacia una llaga
atajas el color de la noche y libertas a los prisioneros

ah para qué alargaron la tierra
del lado en que te miro y no estás niña mía
entre sombra y sombra destino de naufragio
nada tengo oh soledad

sin embargo eres la luz distante que ilumina las frutas
y moriremos juntos
pensar que estás ahí navío blanco listo para partir
y que tenemos juntas las manos en la proa navío siempre en viaje

esta es mi casa
aún la perfuman los bosques
desde donde la acarreaban
allí tricé mi corazón como el espejo para andar a través de mi mismo

esa es la alta ventana y ahí quedan las puertas
de quién fue el hacha que rompió los troncos
tal vez el viento colgó de las vigas
su peso profundo olvidándolo entonces
era cuando la noche bailaba entre sus redes
cuando el niño despertó sollozando
yo no cuento yo digo en palabras desgraciadas
aún los andamios dividen el crepúsculo
y detrás de los vidrios la luz del petróleo
era para mirar hacia el cielo
caía la lluvia en pétalos de vidrio
ahí seguiste el camino que iba a la tempestad
como las altas insistencias del mar
aíslan las piedras duras de las orillas del aire
qué quisiste qué ponías como muriendo muchas veces
todas las cosas suben a un gran silencio
y él se desesperaba inclinado en su borde
sostenías una flor dolorosa
entre sus pétalos giraban los días margaritas de pilotos decaídos

decaído desocupado revolviste de la sombra
el metal de las últimas distancias o esperabas el turno
amaneció sin embargo en los relojes de la tierra
de pronto los días trepan a los años
he aquí tu corazón andando estás cansado sosteniéndote
a tu lado se despiden los pájaros de la estación ausente

admitiendo el cielo profundamente mirando el cielo estoy pensando
con inseguridad sentado en ese borde
oh cielo tejido con aguas y papeles
comencé a hablarme en voz baja decidido a no salir

arrastrado por la respiración de mis raíces
inmóvil navío ávido de esas leguas azules
temblabas y los peces comenzaron a seguirte
tirabas a cantar con grandeza ese instante de sed querías cantar
querías cantar sentado en tu habitación ese día
pero el aire estaba frío en tu corazón como en una campana
un cordel delirante iba a romper tu frío
se me durmió una pierna en esa posición y hablé con ella
cantándole mi alma me pertenece
el cielo era una gota que sonaba cayendo en la gran soledad
pongo el oído y el tiempo como un eucaliptus
frenéticamente canta de lado a lado
en el que estuviera silvando un ladrón
ay y en el límite me paré caballo de las barrancas
sobresaltado ansioso inmóvil sin orinar
en ese instante lo juro oh atardecer que llegas pescador satisfecho
tu canasto vivo en la debilidad del cielo

a quién compré en esta noche la soledad que poseo
quién dice la orden que apresure la marcha
del viento flor de frío entre las hojas inconclusas
si tú me llamas tormenta resuenas tan lejos como un tren

ola triste caída a mis pies quién te dice
sonámbulo de sangre partía cada vez en busca del alba

a ti te reconozco pero lejos apartada
inclinado en tus ojos busco el ancla perdida
ahí la tienes florida adentro de los brazos de nácar
es para terminar para no seguir nunca
y por eso te alabo seguidora de mi alma mirándote hacia atrás
te busco cada vez entre los signos del regreso
estás llena de pájaros durmiendo como el silencio de los bosques
pesado y triste lirio miras hacia otra parte
cuando te hablo me dueles tan distante mujer mía
apresura el paso apresura el paso y enciende las luciérnagas

veo una abeja rondando no existe esa abeja ahora
pequeña mosca con patas lacres mientras golpes cada vez tu vuelo
inclino la cabeza desvalidamente
sigo un cordón que marca siquiera una presencia una situación cual-
[quiera

oigo adornarse el silencio con olas sucesivas
revuelven vuelven ecos aturdidos entonces canto en alta voz
párate sombra de estrella en las cejas de un hombre a la vuelta de
[un camino
que lleva a la espalda una mujer pálida de oro parecida a sí misma
todo está perdido las semanas están cerradas
veo dirigirse el viento con un propósito seguro
como una flor que debe perfumar
abro el otoño taciturno visito la situación de los naufragios
en el fondo del cielo entonces aparecen los pájaros como letras
y el alba se divisa apenas como la cáscara de un fruto
o es que entonces sumerges tus pies en otra distancia
el día es de fuego y se apuntala en sus colores
el mar lleno de trapos verdes sus salivas murmullan soy el mar
el movimiento atraído la inquieta caja
tengo fresca el alma con todas mis respiraciones
ahí sofoco al lado de las noches antárticas
me pongo la luna como una flor de jacinto la moja mi lágrima lúgubre
ahíto estoy y anda mi vida con todos los pies parecidos

crío el sobresalto me lleno de terror transparente
estoy solo en una pieza sin ventanas
sin tener qué hacer con los itinerarios extraviados
veo llenarse de caracoles las paredes como orillas de buques
pego la cara a ellas absorto profundamente
siguiendo un reloj no amando la noche quiero que pase
con su tejido de culebra con luces
guirnalda de fríos mi cinturón da vuelta muchas veces
soy la yegua que sola galopa perdidamente a la siga del alba muy
[triste
agujero sin cesar cuando acompaño con mi sordera estremeciéndose
saltan como elásticos o peces los habitantes acostados
mis alas absorben como el pabellón de un parque con olvido
amanecen los puertos como herraduras abandonadas
ay me sorprendo canto en la carpa delirante
como un equilibrista enamorado o el primer pescador
pobre hombre que aíslas temblando como una gota
un cuadrado de tiempo completamente inmóvil

el mes de junio se extendió de repente en el tiempo con seriedad y
[exactitud
como un caballo y en el relámpago crucé la orilla
ay el crujir del aire pacífico era muy grande
los cinematógrafos desocupados el color de los cementerios

los buques destruidos las tristezas
encima de los follajes
encima de las astas de las vacas la noche tirante su trapo bailando
el movimiento rápido del día igual al de las manos que detienen un
[vehículo

yo asustado comía
oh lluvia que creces como las plantas oh victrolas ensimismadas
personas de corazón voluntarioso todo lo celebré
en un tren de satisfacciones desde donde mi retrato
tiene detrás el mundo que describo con pasión
los árboles interesantes como periódicos los caseríos los rieles
ay el lugar decaído en que el arco iris
deja su pollera enredada al huir
todo como los poetas los filósofos las parejas que se aman
yo lo comienzo a celebrar entusiasta sencillo
yo tengo la alegría de los panaderos contentos y entonces
amanecía débilmente con un color de violín
con un sonido de campana con el olor de la larga distancia

devuélveme la grande rosa la sed traída al mundo
a donde voy supongo iguales las cosas
la noche importante y triste y ahí mi querella
barcarolero de las largas aguas cuando

de pronto una gaviota crece en tus sienes mi corazón está cansado
márcame tu pata gris llena de lejos
tu viaje de la orilla del mar amargo o espérame
el baho se despierta como una violeta es que
a tu árbol noche querida sube un niño
a robarse las frutas
y los lagartos brotan de tu pesada vestidura
entonces el día salta encima de su abeja
estoy de pie en la luz como el medio día en la tierra
quiero contarlo todo con ternura
centinela de las malas estaciones ahí estás tú
pescador intranquilo déjame adornarte por ejemplo
un cinturón de frutas dulce la melancolía
espérame donde voy ah el atardecer
la comida las barcarolas del océano oh espérame
adelantándote como un grito atrasándote como una huella oh
                                                              [espérate
sentado en esa última sombra o todavía después
todavía

INDEX OF FIRST LINES ENGLISH/SPANISH

pale blazes twisting at the edge of night
hogueras pálidas revolviéndose al borde de las noches

city from the hills at night the harvesters sleep
ciudad desde los cerros en la noche los segadores duermen

city from the hills through the leafy night
ciudad desde los cerros entre la noche de hojas

stretched out in the grass my heart is sad
tendido sobre el pasto mi corazón está triste

oh coiled thickets towards which sleep advances trains
oh matorrales crespos adonde el sueño avanza trenes

its momentum rising a wing passes by a flight oh night without keys
alza su empuje un ala pasa un vuelo oh noche sin llaves

star suspended between the thick night the days of tall sails
estrella retardada entre la noche gruesa los días de altas velas

beholding you then the bold ones leap forth you climb to the lights
    migrating
divisándote entonces resaltan las audaces te trepas a las luces emigrando

i twist this hostile undergrowth this rocking chair for birds
tuerzo esta hostil maleza mecedora de los pájaros

i claw this bark i destroy the stalks of grass
araño esta corteza destrozo los ramales de la hierba

i do not know how to sing of the daytime
no sé hacer el canto de los días

big ships of embers twist their green sails
tuercen sus velas verdes grandes buques de brasa

twisting to that side or beyond you continue being mine
torciendo hacia ese lado o más allá continúas siendo mía

a gesture of joy a word of sorrow that i were closer to you
un gesto de alegría una palabra de pena que estuviera más cerca de ti

when i draw the sky near with my hands to fully awaken
cuando aproximo el cielo con las manos para despertar completamente

every time every time to the north are the unfinished cities
cada vez cada vez al norte están las ciudades inconclusas

right beside me young woman in love
al lado de mí mismo señorita enamorada

i am the one who plucks names and high constellations of dew
yo soy el que deshoja nombres y altas constelaciones de rocío

and yet you are the distant light that illuminates the fruit
sin embargo eres la luz distante que ilumina las frutas

this is my house
esta es mi casa

that is the high window and there are the doors
esa es la alta ventana y ahí quedan las puertas

dispirited vacant did you wrest from the shadows
decaído desocupado revolviste de la sombra

letting the sky in deeply watching the sky i am thinking
admitiendo el cielo profundamente mirando el cielo estoy pensando

drawn down by the respiration of my roots
arrastrado por la respiración de mis raíces

for whom did i buy the solitude i possess tonight
a quién compré en esta noche la soledad que poseo

sad wave fallen at my feet who calls you
ola triste caída a mis pies quién te dice

i see a bee circling this bee does not exist now
veo una abeja rondando no existe esa abeja ahora

i hear the silence adorn itself with successive waves
oigo adornarse el silencio con olas sucesivas

i beget fright i am filled with transparent terror
crío el sobresalto me lleno de terror transparente

the month of june stretched out suddenly in time with seriousness
and exactitude
*el mes de junio se extendió de repente en el tiempo con seriedad y
exactitud*

the ruined ships the sorrows
los buques destruidos las tristezas

give me back the great rose the thirst brought to the world
devuélveme la grande rosa la sed traída al mundo

suddenly a seagull grows upon your brow my heart is weary
de pronto una gaviota crece en tus sienes mi corazón está cansado